TURKEY THROUGH THE AGES

A CONCISE GUIDE

By

Martin Miller-Yianni

The Emblem of Turkey

COPYRIGHT AND ACKNOWLEDGEMENTS

Publisher: Martin Miller-Yianni, Yambol, Bulgaria

First Printed Edition 2023

ISBN 978-619-7742-29-9 (paperback)

ISBN 978-619-7742-30-5 (e-book ePub)

A CIP catalogue record for this book is available from:

The National Register of Published Books in Bulgaria

bulevard 'Vasil Levski' 88,

1504 Sofia,

Bulgaria

Cover Photograph (Suleymaniye Mosque, İstanbul) by Ivan Alekslc from Unsplash.com

CONTENTS

INTRODUCTION

"Turkey Through the Ages: A Concise Guide" serves as a valuable reference for students, inquisitive travellers, and those intrigued by the captivating history of Turkey. This book is part of a series of books about various countries. The book's well-organised structure and clear presentation facilitate easy navigation through various historical periods, allowing readers to swiftly locate specific information.

From the ancient civilisations of Turkey to contemporary developments, this book comprehensively covers essential facets of Turkey's history. It enables readers to grasp the historical context and cultural heritage of the region. The concise format makes it an ideal choice for those seeking a quick reference or an introduction to Turkey's past.

Presented in a readable and accessible British English style, the book offers a comprehensive overview without compromising on accuracy or depth. This quality makes it an excellent resource for gaining knowledge about Turkey's diverse historical foundations.

It's worth noting that some chapters may recap and explain important events as in previous chapters. Such recapitulations are inevitable, as era transitions often share events and important figures, reinforcing the interconnectedness of Turkey's history. They serve as valuable reminders, aiding in comprehending the broader historical narrative.

Whether you aim to refresh your knowledge of a specific historical era or develop a general understanding of Turkey's past, this book delivers reliable information and serves as an invaluable guide. It immerses readers in the triumphs, challenges, and cultural metamorphoses that have contributed to Turkey's identity, offering a fascinating journey through time.

This book stands as an engaging and informative read that provides a succinct yet comprehensive look at Turkey's history. It remains an exceptional resource for anyone eager to explore the fascinating story of this region and gain a deeper appreciation for its rich cultural heritage.

The Turkish flag boasts a distinctive and impactful design that encapsulates the essence of the nation's rich history and cultural heritage. It features a red background with a white star and crescent in the centre. This design holds deep historical and cultural significance for Turkey, representing key elements of its identity.

The red background symbolises the blood shed by those who fought for the country's independence, while the white star and crescent are associated with Islam, reflecting Turkey's historical and cultural ties to the Ottoman Empire. The crescent moon, a common symbol in Islamic iconography, is also indicative of Turkey's predominantly Muslim population.

Officially adopted on June 5, 1936, the Turkish flag is a source of immense pride for the Turkish people. Its symbolism goes beyond aesthetics, serving as a visual representation of Turkey's enduring spirit, cultural heritage, and the values that have shaped the nation throughout its history. The flag, with its evocative design and historical resonance, stands as a powerful emblem of Turkish unity and identity.

THE LOCATION OF TURKEY

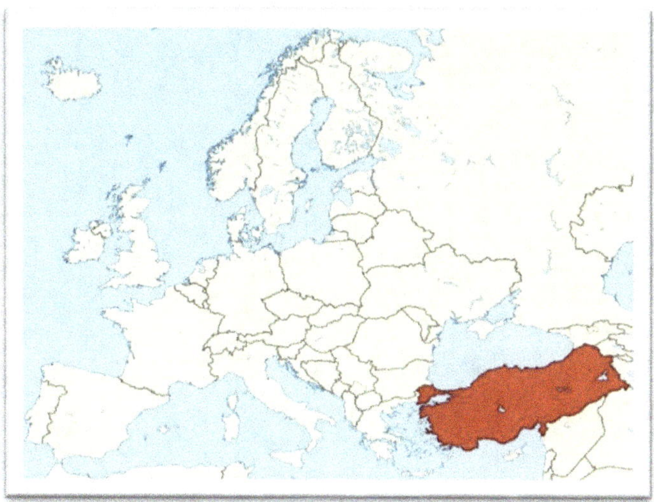

Turkey, spanning approximately 783,356 square kilometres, holds a strategic location at the crossroads of Europe and Asia, positioned at the meeting point of the continents. The country's diverse geography encompasses various features, including mountainous regions like the Taurus Mountains and Mount Ararat, expansive plateaus, and a substantial coastline along the Aegean, Mediterranean, and Black Seas.

The extensive coastline, flanked by the Aegean Sea to the west, the Mediterranean Sea to the south, and the Black Sea to the north, has significantly shaped Turkey's cultural and economic activities throughout history.

Turkey shares its land borders with several countries, fostering historical connections and cultural exchanges. It is bordered by Greece to the west, Bulgaria to the northwest, Georgia to the northeast, Armenia, Azerbaijan, and Iran to the east, and Iraq and Syria to the south. These geopolitical connections have played a vital role in shaping Turkey's history and influencing its cultural diversity.

The country is traversed by numerous rivers, including the Euphrates and Tigris, contributing to its varied landscapes and agricultural productivity. The climate in Turkey ranges from Mediterranean along the coastal areas to continental in the interior and eastern regions.

In the heart of the Anatolian peninsula, a cradle of human civilisation, the ages of history unfold through thousands of years. This ancient land, encompassing what is now modern-day Turkey, stands as a testament to the enduring spirit of humanity. From the Neolithic era to the Hellenistic period, a rich network of diverse civilisations has flourished, each leaving an indelible mark on the landscape.

The journey begins around 40,000 years ago when the first inhabitants settled in Eastern Thrace, the European part of Turkey. Neolithic settlements such as Göbekli Tepe and Çatalhöyük emerged as beacons of human progress. Göbekli Tepe, with its enigmatic stone pillars dating back to 9600 B.C., is a testament to communal gatherings, possibly of a religious nature. Meanwhile, Çatalhöyük, a sprawling Neolithic settlement from 7500 B.C., unveils the transition from nomadic life to settled agricultural communities. Here, ancient residents cultivated cereals, herded sheep and cattle, and crafted intricate pottery and tools.

Around 2300 B.C., the Hattians and Hurrians were early stewards of Anatolia. The Indo-European Hittites gradually assimilated the Hattians and Hurrians from 2000 to 1700 B.C., establishing the region's first empire. The Hittite Empire, reaching its height under Suppiluliuma I in the 14th century B.C., showcased military might and diplomatic finesse. Hattusa, the grand *capital adorned with temples and palaces, echoed with the worship of a diverse pantheon. Yet, like all great empires, the Hittites faced eventual decline, succumbing to internal strife and external pressures around 1180 B.C.

The Göbekli Tepe Stone Pillars

Following the Hittite era, the Phrygians emerged around the 12th century B.C., establishing their kingdom in central Anatolia. Gordium, their capital, would forever be linked to the legendary Gordian Knot. The Lydians, cantered around Sardis, ushered in an economic renaissance, being credited as the first civilisation to mint coins. Their interactions with Greek city-states and the Persian Empire played a pivotal role in shaping the geopolitical landscape.

In the rugged beauty of the Lake Van region, the Urartians thrived from the 9th to the 6th centuries B.C. Known for advanced fortifications and irrigation systems, the Urartians left monumental fortresses adorned with intricate carvings. Despite their eventual decline, the echoes of Urartian achievements reverberated through subsequent cultures.

As the 6th century B.C. dawned, the Armenian Orontid dynasty took root in eastern Turkey, adding another chapter to Anatolia's storied history. The Aeolian and Ionian Greeks, drawn by the allure of the Anatolian coast, founded cities like Miletus, Ephesus, and Byzantium, contributing to the region's cultural mosaic.

During this era, notable figures such as King Suppiluliuma I of the Hittites, the legendary Gordius of Gordium, and the innovative Lydian King Alyattes, who played a pivotal role in the economic resurgence, left their mark on Anatolian history. Events such as the decline of the Hittite Empire and the formation of the Urartian civilisation added layers of complexity to historical archives.

The ancient times of Anatolia, woven with threads of Neolithic innovation, Hittite grandeur, and the contributions of Phrygians, Lydians, and Urartians, tell a captivating tale. It is a narrative of human resilience, cultural exchange, and the ever-evolving dance between civilisations. In the corridors of time, Anatolia stands as a living testament to the enduring spirit of humanity, where the echoes of the past resonate in the present, and the vibrant history of the region continues to inspire awe and fascination.

Göbekli Tepe (Neolithic era): Enigmatic stone pillars dating back to 9600 B.C., possibly used for communal gatherings of a religious nature.

Çatalhöyük (Neolithic era): Sprawling Neolithic settlement from 7500 B.C., revealing the transition from nomadic life to settled agricultural communities. Residents cultivated cereals, herded sheep and cattle, and crafted intricate pottery and tools.

Hattians and Hurrians (2300 B.C.): Early stewards of Anatolia before the Indo-European Hittites assimilated them from 2000 to 1700 B.C.

Hittite Empire (2000–1180 B.C.): Established by the Indo-European Hittites, reaching its peak under Suppiluliuma I in the 14th century B.C. Hattusa, the grand capital, adorned with temples and palaces, showcased military might and diplomatic finesse.

Phrygians (12th century B.C.): Emerged and established their kingdom in central Anatolia, with Gordium as their capital, forever linked to the legendary Gordian Knot.

Urartians (9th–6th centuries B.C.): Thrived in the rugged beauty of the Lake Van region, known for advanced fortifications and irrigation systems. Left monumental fortresses adorned with intricate carvings.

Armenian Orontid dynasty (6th century B.C.): Took root in eastern Turkey, adding another chapter to Anatolia's storied history.

Aeolian and Ionian Greeks (6th century B.C.): Founded cities like Miletus, Ephesus, and Byzantium on the Anatolian coast, contributing to the region's cultural mosaic.

Gordius of Gordium (12th century B.C.): Linked to the legendary Gordian Knot, adding a mythical aspect to Anatolian history.

King Suppiluliuma I of the Hittites (14th century B.C.): Led the Hittite Empire to its height, showcasing military might and diplomatic finesse.

King Alyattes of Lydia (6th century B.C.): Innovative Lydian king who played a pivotal role in the economic resurgence of the region.

Decline of the Hittite Empire (1180 B.C.): The great empire succumbed to internal strife and external pressures.

Formation of the Urartian civilisation (9th century B.C.): Marked by advanced fortifications and irrigation systems in the Lake Van region.

As the 6th century B.C. dawned, Lydia, under the reign of King Croesus, stood as a testament to wealth and splendour. Sardis, the capital, glistened as a jewel in Lydia's crown, radiating cultural vibrancy across the landscape.

The Persian Empire, led by the formidable Cyrus the Great, swept through Anatolia in 546 B.C., bringing Lydia under its dominion. Darius I, an architect of imperial expansion, extended Persian control, leaving the monumental city of Persepolis as an enduring symbol of their might.

Amidst this imperial dominance, Miletus, an Ionian city, became the crucible of dissent, sparking the Ionian Revolt against Persian rule. The reverberations of this rebellion echoed through the ages, culminating in the heroic stand of Anatolian Greeks at the Battle of Marathon in 490 B.C.

The Peloponnesian War (431–404 B.C.) unfolded as Athens and Sparta vied for supremacy, turning Anatolia into a theatre of conflict where the ebb and flow of power played out across its cities.

Enter Alexander the Great, whose conquests reshaped Anatolia's destiny. The Battle of Granicus in 334 B.C. marked a turning point, leading to the enigmatic confrontation with the Gordian Knot in Gordion, a prelude to Alexander's relentless march.

Alexander the Great Cutting the Gordian Knot

In the Hellenistic aftermath of Alexander's demise, Anatolia fell under the sway of the Seleucid Empire. Pergamon emerged as a beacon of Hellenistic brilliance, contributing to the rich cultural makeup with its architectural achievements.

Thus, Anatolia's past, marked by Lydia's opulence, Persian dominion, Ionian revolt, Peloponnesian struggles, Alexander's conquests, and Hellenistic glory, weaves a continuous narrative that echoes through the corridors of time.

During the Hellenistic period in Turkey, spanning from the late 4th to the 1st century B.C., the region experienced a profound transformation under the influence of Hellenistic culture following the conquests of Alexander the Great. This era marked a captivating fusion of Greek and Anatolian civilisations, giving rise to rich cultural, artistic, and architectural developments.

Alexander's conquest of Anatolia in the 4th century B.C. paved the way for the establishment of Hellenistic city-states. Cities such as Ephesus, Pergamon, and Antioch flourished as hubs of intellectual exchange and artistic innovation. The architectural landscape saw the emergence of grandiose structures, adorned with intricate columns and statues, showcasing the mastery of Greek artisans.

The Hellenistic rulers who succeeded Alexander, such as the Seleucids and the Attalids, played a pivotal role in shaping the political landscape of the region. Pergamon, under the Attalid dynasty, became a beacon of cultural brilliance, boasting the renowned Library of Pergamum, rivalling even the Library of Alexandria. This intellectual flourishing contributed to the advancement of knowledge in various fields, from philosophy to medicine.

Art during this period reflected a harmonious blend of Greek and Anatolian influences. The famed Altar of Zeus in Pergamon, an exquisite masterpiece of Hellenistic sculpture, stands as a testament to the artistic prowess of the era. The Anatolian penchant for intricate details merged seamlessly with the Greek idealism, creating sculptures that evoke a sense of awe and wonder.

Altar of Zeus in Pergamon

Trade and commerce thrived, facilitated by the interconnectedness of the Hellenistic world. The bustling city of Ephesus, adorned with the grandeur of the Temple of Artemis, served as a vital trading hub, connecting the East and West. The agora, with its vibrant markets, echoed with the diverse languages and cultures of merchants from across the Mediterranean.

However, the Hellenistic period in Turkey was not without its challenges. The constant power struggles among the successor states and the encroachment of the Roman Republic in the 2nd century B.C. ushered in a new era, ultimately leading to the absorption of Anatolia into the Roman Empire. Despite this geopolitical shift, the legacy of the Hellenistic period endured, leaving an indelible imprint on the cultural fabric of Turkey.

The Hellenistic period in Turkey stands as a captivating chapter in history, where the interplay of Greek and Anatolian elements created a myriad of cultural brilliance. The architectural marvels, artistic achievements, and intellectual pursuits of this era continue to resonate, weaving a narrative that transcends time.

King Croesus of Lydia (6th century B.C.): Lydia, under his reign, stood as a testament to wealth and splendour. Sardis, the capital, glistened as a jewel in Lydia's crown, radiating cultural vibrancy across the landscape.

Cyrus the Great (546 B.C.): Led the Persian Empire, sweeping through Anatolia and bringing Lydia under its dominion.

Darius I (circa 500 B.C.): Extended Persian control, leaving the monumental city of Persepolis as an enduring symbol of their might.

Ionian Revolt (circa 499–494 B.C.): Miletus, an Ionian city, became the crucible of dissent, sparking the Ionian Revolt against Persian rule. The Battle of Marathon in 490 B.C. was a culmination of the rebellion.

Peloponnesian War (431–404 B.C.): Unfolded as Athens and Sparta vied for supremacy, turning Anatolia into a theatre of conflict.

Alexander the Great (334 B.C.): Conquests reshaped Anatolia's destiny. The Battle of Granicus marked a turning point, leading to the enigmatic confrontation with the Gordian Knot in Gordion.

Hellenistic period in Turkey (Late 4th to 1st century B.C.): Marked by the fusion of Greek and Anatolian civilisations following Alexander the Great's conquests.

Ephesus, Pergamon, and Antioch (4th century B.C.): Hellenistic city-states flourished as hubs of intellectual exchange and artistic innovation.

Seleucid Empire (Hellenistic period): Anatolia fell under its sway in the Hellenistic aftermath of Alexander's demise.

Attalid dynasty (Hellenistic period): Pergamon emerged as a beacon of Hellenistic brilliance, boasting the renowned Library of Pergamum.

Library of Pergamum (Hellenistic period): Rivalling the Library of Alexandria, it contributed to the advancement of knowledge in various fields.

Altar of Zeus in Pergamon (Hellenistic period): Exquisite masterpiece of Hellenistic sculpture, reflecting a harmonious blend of Greek and Anatolian influences.

Trade and commerce (Hellenistic period): Thrived, facilitated by the interconnectedness of the Hellenistic world. Ephesus served as a vital trading hub.

Power struggles among successor states (Hellenistic period): Constant conflicts among Hellenistic rulers and the encroachment of the Roman Republic in the 2nd century B.C.

Absorption of Anatolia into the Roman Empire (2nd century B.C.): Resulted from geopolitical shifts, ending the Hellenistic period in Turkey.

Legacy of the Hellenistic period (Ongoing): Endured, leaving an indelible imprint on the cultural fabric of Turkey, with architectural marvels, artistic achievements, and intellectual pursuits continuing to resonate.

During the period spanning 334 B.C. to the 1st century B.C., the region now known as Turkey witnessed significant historical events, marked predominantly by the conquests of Alexander the Great and the subsequent Hellenistic period.

In 334 B.C., Alexander the Great crossed into Asia Minor, initiating a series of military campaigns that would reshape the geopolitical landscape. The Battle of Granicus in 334 B.C. marked the beginning of his conquests in the region, leading to the establishment of Hellenistic influence.

Alexander's conquests brought about the fusion of Greek and Persian cultures, a phenomenon known as Hellenisation. Cities were founded, often named after the conqueror, such as Alexandria Troas. This cultural amalgamation had a profound and lasting impact on the Anatolian Peninsula.

Following Alexander's death in 323 B.C., his vast empire was divided among his generals, leading to the formation of the Seleucid Empire, Ptolemaic Kingdom, and the Antigonid dynasty. The Diadochi, as these successors were known, engaged in power struggles that extended into Asia Minor.

The Kingdom of Pontus, under Mithridates VI, played a prominent role during the 1st century B.C. Mithridates, known for his resistance against Roman expansion, engaged in a series of conflicts with the Roman Republic, culminating in the three Mithridatic Wars.

Mithridates VI

One of the most notable events during this period was the Mithridatic Wars (88–63 B.C.), where Rome and Pontus clashed for control over the Anatolian region. The Roman general Lucius Cornelius Sulla's campaigns and the subsequent campaigns of Gnaeus Pompeius Magnus contributed to the Roman dominance in Asia Minor.

The 1st century B.C. saw the gradual incorporation of Anatolia into the Roman Republic and later the Roman Empire. The region became a vital part of the Roman province of Asia, contributing to the cultural, economic, and political integration of Anatolia into the Roman world.

The period from 334 B.C. to the 1st century B.C. in the history of Turkey was marked by the conquests of Alexander the Great, the Hellenistic influence, and the subsequent interactions with the Roman Republic. These events laid the foundations for the rich historical background of Anatolia, shaping its destiny for centuries to come.

Alexander the Great's Conquests (334 B.C.): Crossing into Asia Minor, he initiated a series of military campaigns, beginning with the Battle of Granicus. The conquests reshaped the geopolitical landscape and marked the start of Hellenistic influence.

Hellenisation (334–323 B.C.): Alexander's conquests led to the fusion of Greek and Persian cultures. Cities, including Alexandria Troas, were founded, influencing the Anatolian Peninsula profoundly.

Division of Alexander's Empire (323 B.C.): Following Alexander's death, his generals, known as the Diadochi, formed the Seleucid Empire, Ptolemaic Kingdom, and the Antigonid dynasty. Power struggles among the Diadochi extended into Asia Minor.

Kingdom of Pontus under Mithridates VI (1st century B.C.): Played a prominent role and resisted Roman expansion, engaging in the three Mithridatic Wars against the Roman Republic.

Mithridatic Wars (88–63 B.C.): Rome and Pontus clashed for control over Anatolia. Lucius Cornelius Sulla's campaigns and subsequent actions by Gnaeus Pompeius Magnus contributed to Roman dominance in Asia Minor.

Incorporation of Anatolia into the Roman Republic and Empire (1st century B.C.): The gradual integration of Anatolia into the Roman province of Asia, contributing to cultural, economic, and political ties with the Roman world.

Roman Province of Asia (1st century B.C.): Anatolia became a vital part of the Roman Republic and later the Roman Empire, shaping its destiny for centuries to come.

The period from 334 B.C. to the 1st century B.C. in the history of Turkey was marked by the conquests of Alexander the Great, the Hellenistic influence, and subsequent interactions with the Roman Republic. These events laid the foundations for the rich historical verses of Anatolia, shaping its destiny for centuries to come.

Galatia, situated in central Anatolia, was initially inhabited by Celts before undergoing Hellenisation and being known as Hellenogalatai. The Kingdom of Pontus, a Hellenistic realm, emerged in 281 B.C. and endured until Roman conquest in 63 B.C. Gradually, all regions corresponding to modern-day Turkey became integral parts of the Roman Empire, retaining their historical designations as Roman provinces. In 330 A.D., Constantinople (present-day Istanbul) assumed the role of the new Roman capital, marking a momentous historical shift.

The Acts of Apostles document the Christian and Roman period in the Anatolian region. Antioch, located in southern Turkey (now Antakya), holds significance as the birthplace where followers of Jesus were first called "Christians." The city swiftly evolved into a major centre for Christianity. The Apostle Paul of Tarsus journeyed to Ephesus, residing there and engaging in tentmaking. Ephesus witnessed notable events, including miracles attributed to Paul, although he eventually left due to opposition from a local silversmith, leading to a pro-Artemis riot.

Extrabiblical traditions assert that the Assumption of Mary took place in Ephesus, where Apostle John was also present. Irenaeus mentions the church of Ephesus, founded by Paul, with John's continued involvement. Apostle John authored three epistles during his time in Ephesus. The Basilica of St.

John, constructed by Justinian the Great in the 6th century, marks the burial site of Apostle John. Nearby, the House of the Virgin Mary is acknowledged by the Catholic Church as the place where Mary, mother of Jesus, spent her final days before her Assumption. Saint Nicholas, born in Patara, resided in Myra (modern Demre) in Lycia.

Burial Site of Apostle John in Ephesus

In 123 A.D., the Roman Emperor Hadrian visited Anatolia, resulting in the erection of numerous monuments. Hadrian focused on Greek revival, enhancing cities like Cyzicus, Pergamon, Smyrna, Ephesus, and Sardes as regional centres for the Imperial cult.

Transitioning into the Byzantine period, Constantine the Great, after defeating Licinius, selected Byzantium as the new capital of the Roman Empire. In 330, he officially proclaimed it New Rome (Nova Roma), later renaming it Constantinople. Though Christianity did not become the state's official religion under Constantine, it enjoyed imperial preference.

Medallion of Constantine the Great

Theodosius the Great established Christianity as the official state religion in 380. Following Theodosius's death in 395, Constantinople became the capital of the Eastern Roman Empire, later known as the Byzantine Empire.

In the 2nd century B.C., Anatolia became a significant part of the expanding Roman Republic, marking a transformative period in the region's history. The incorporation of Anatolia into the Roman Republic brought about changes in governance, culture, and society.

The Roman Republic's involvement in Anatolia began with the bequest of the Kingdom of Pergamon to Rome by King Attalus III in 133 B.C. This act laid the groundwork for Roman control and influence in the region. The Roman Republic, eager to assert its dominance in the eastern Mediterranean, gradually extended its authority over various Anatolian territories.

One of the key figures in this process was the Roman general Lucius Cornelius Sulla, who secured Roman control over much of Anatolia in the mid-1st century B.C. The region became a vital part of Rome's efforts to consolidate power in the eastern Mediterranean.

Roman General Lucius Cornelius Sulla

The Roman presence brought about administrative changes in Anatolia. The province of Asia, encompassing western Anatolia, became one of the first senatorial provinces, administered by proconsuls appointed by the Roman Senate. This administrative structure aimed to integrate the newly acquired territories into the Roman political system.

Cities in Anatolia, such as Ephesus, continued to thrive under Roman rule. The Romans made significant contributions to the region's infrastructure, constructing roads, aqueducts, and public buildings. The Roman cultural influence, including the Latin language and Roman legal traditions, began to permeate Anatolian society.

Anatolia's strategic importance was further underscored by the construction of the Via Egnatia, a major Roman road connecting Byzantium (later Constantinople) to Dyrrhachium (modern Durrës). This road facilitated trade, communication, and the movement of Roman legions.

The spread of Christianity also gained momentum during the Roman Republic's rule in Anatolia. The Apostle Paul's missionary journeys, as documented in the New Testament, included visits to cities like Ephesus and Corinth, contributing to the early Christian communities in the region.

As the Roman Republic transitioned into the Roman Empire, Anatolia remained a crucial part of the imperial structure. The region's prosperity and strategic importance continued, and its cultural and historical significance persisted through subsequent centuries.

The integration of Anatolia into the Roman Republic in the 2nd century B.C. marked a pivotal moment in the region's history.

The Roman influence brought about changes in governance, infrastructure, and culture, laying the foundation for Anatolia's enduring connection with the Roman Empire.

The transition from the Roman Republic to the Byzantine Empire marked a significant shift in Anatolia's history, shaping its political, cultural, and religious landscape. The establishment of the Byzantine Empire, often considered the continuation of the Eastern Roman Empire, brought about enduring changes that would influence the region for centuries.

By the 4th century A.D., the Roman Empire had undergone significant administrative reforms, with the capital moving eastward to Byzantium, later known as Constantinople. This city, strategically positioned on the border between Europe and Asia, became a symbol of the Byzantine Empire's power and cultural richness.

Under Emperor Constantine the Great, who officially founded Constantinople in 330 A.D., the Eastern Roman Empire emerged as a distinct entity from the Western Roman Empire. Constantinople's status as the new capital reinforced Anatolia's centrality in the Byzantine state.

Anatolia played a crucial role in the defence of the Byzantine Empire against external threats, including invasions by various Germanic and Turkic tribes. The construction of the Theodosian Walls around Constantinople exemplifies the importance placed on securing the empire's eastern frontier.

The Byzantine Empire, often referred to as Byzantium or the Eastern Roman Empire, embraced Christianity as its official religion under Emperor Constantine. This had a profound impact on Anatolia, as the region became a centre for Christian theology, monasticism, and ecclesiastical architecture. Iconic structures like Hagia Sophia in Constantinople and the rock-cut churches of Cappadocia reflect the Byzantine influence on Anatolian religious and architectural traditions.

Hagia Sophia in Constantinople

Anatolia was not only a cultural and religious centre but also a hub of economic activity during the Byzantine period. Cities such as Ephesus and Thessaloniki maintained their prominence as commercial and trade centres, facilitating the flow of goods between East and West.

Despite the cultural and economic prosperity, the Byzantine Empire faced numerous challenges, including conflicts with the Sassanian Empire, Arab invasions, and internal struggles. The Byzantines managed to endure for nearly a millennium, but the empire eventually succumbed to the Ottoman Turks in 1453, marking the end of the Byzantine era.

The Byzantine Empire's succession of the Roman Empire in Anatolia had profound and lasting effects on the region. The establishment of Constantinople as the Byzantine capital, the promotion of Christianity, and the cultural and economic vibrancy of Anatolian cities all contributed to shaping the historical narrative of the region during this significant period.

Emperor Constantine the Great (c. 272–337): Constantine played a pivotal role in the establishment of Constantinople as the new capital and the official proclamation of Christianity as the state religion.

Theodosian Walls (5th century): Constructed to fortify Constantinople against external threats, the Theodosian Walls highlighted the strategic importance of Anatolia in defending the Byzantine Empire.

Hagia Sophia (537): The construction of the Hagia Sophia in Constantinople under Emperor Justinian I became an iconic symbol of Byzantine architecture and Christianity.

Rock-cut churches of Cappadocia: Reflecting the Byzantine influence on religious traditions, the rock-cut churches in Cappadocia showcased unique architectural and artistic expressions.

Germanic and Turkic Invasions: Anatolia played a crucial role in the defence against invasions by Germanic and Turkic tribes during the Byzantine period.

Sassanian Empire and Arab Invasions: The Byzantine Empire faced conflicts with the Sassanian Empire and Arab invasions, influencing the political dynamics of Anatolia.

Economic Centres: Cities like Ephesus and Thessaloniki continued to thrive as economic and trade centres, contributing to the prosperity of the Byzantine Empire.

Ottoman Conquest (1453): The fall of Constantinople to the Ottoman Turks in 1453 marked the end of the Byzantine Empire and the beginning of a new chapter in Anatolian history.

Legacy of Byzantine Influence: The Byzantine Empire's influence on Anatolian culture, architecture, and Christianity persisted even after its collapse, leaving a lasting legacy.

Christian Theology and Monasticism: Anatolia became a significant centre for Christian theology and monasticism during the Byzantine period, contributing to the development of religious traditions.

Commercial and Trade Networks: Byzantine cities in Anatolia maintained their importance in commercial and trade networks, connecting the East and West.

The transition from the Roman Empire to the Byzantine Empire in Anatolia marked a complex and transformative period. The strategic significance of Anatolia, the establishment of Constantinople, and the cultural, religious, and economic developments during this era laid the foundation for the Byzantine legacy in the region.

4TH CENTURY – 1071

The Byzantine Empire, a formidable power in Europe, governed most of present-day Turkey until the Late Middle Ages. Prolific Byzantine-Sassanid Wars unfolded between the 4th and 7th centuries.

Numerous ecumenical councils convened in present-day Turkey, including the First Council of Nicaea in 325 and the Council of Ephesus in 431. Recognised for its economic, cultural, and military influence, the Byzantine Empire hosted the enduring institution of the Ecumenical Patriarchate of Constantinople in Istanbul.

Shifting to the Great Seljuk Empire, originating from the Oghuz Turks in the 9th century, the Seljuks migrated to Persia, forming the Great Seljuk Empire in the 10th century. In the 11th century, the Seljuks entered medieval Armenia and Anatolia, prevailing over the Byzantines at the Battle of Manzikert in 1071. This event marked the commencement of Turkification, introducing Turkish language and Islam to Anatolia and gradually transforming the region from a Christian and Greek-speaking to a Muslim and Turkish-speaking one.

The relocation of the capital from Rome to Constantinople was a pivotal moment in Byzantine history, bearing profound implications for Anatolia and the broader Eastern Roman world. Initiated by Emperor Constantine the Great in the early 4th century, this move marked the establishment of a new political, cultural, and economic centre.

Strategically positioned on the border between Europe and Asia, Constantinople offered numerous advantages. Its location facilitated control over vital trade routes and provided a robust defensive position against potential invasions. The city's natural harbour, the Golden Horn, burgeoned into a bustling centre for maritime commerce.

Map of Constantinople in 1572

The establishment of Constantinople as the Byzantine capital fostered the city's rapid growth and development. Emperor Constantine embarked on extensive construction projects, transforming the city into a grand metropolis. The most iconic structure from this period is the Hagia Sophia, a monumental cathedral that later became a symbol of Byzantine architecture and Christianity.

Byzantine emperors continued to enhance Constantinople's infrastructure, erecting defensive walls, aqueducts, and public buildings. The Theodosian Walls, constructed during the reign of Theodosius II, played a pivotal role in safeguarding the city against external threats and sieges.

Constantinople's status as the imperial capital elevated its cultural and intellectual significance. The city evolved into a hub for learning, with renowned schools, libraries, and academies attracting scholars from across the empire. The preservation and transmission of classical Greek and Roman knowledge thrived in this intellectual environment.

The Byzantine capital also played a crucial role in the religious history of the Eastern Roman Empire. Constantinople hosted the Ecumenical Councils, addressing theological issues and shaping Christian doctrine. The city's patriarch, as the head of the Eastern Orthodox Church, held a position of great influence.

Economically, Constantinople blossomed into a flourishing centre of trade and commerce. The Byzantine Empire's control over key trade routes facilitated the exchange of goods between Europe, Asia, and the Middle East. The city's markets, including the renowned Grand Bazaar, became celebrated for their diversity and vibrancy.

Despite Constantinople's grandeur, the Byzantine Empire faced numerous challenges, including invasions, internal strife, and economic fluctuations. Nevertheless, the city endured as a symbol of Byzantine strength and resilience for centuries.

The relocation of the capital to Constantinople by Emperor Constantine transformed the Byzantine Empire and left an indelible mark on Anatolia. The city's strategic location, cultural richness, and economic prosperity shaped the course of Byzantine history and contributed to Constantinople's enduring legacy in the annals of world civilisation.

The era characterised by Arab invasions and conflicts with the Seljuk Turks in the later years of the Byzantine Empire profoundly influenced Anatolia, moulding its political, cultural, and demographic landscape.

In the 7th century, the expansion of the Arab Caliphates led to significant military campaigns into Byzantine Anatolia. The Battle of Yarmouk in 636 and the subsequent capture of Jerusalem marked the commencement of Arab incursions into the region. Though Arab conquests in Anatolia were not as extensive as in the Levant, parts of the region experienced Arab rule, contributing to cultural and religious diversity.

The Arab presence left an impact on Anatolia's cultural and linguistic landscape. Some local populations embraced Islam, introducing Arabic as a significant language in the region. However, pockets of resistance persisted, and Anatolia remained a frontier zone with ongoing conflicts between the Byzantines and various Arab dynasties.

The 11th century witnessed the rise of the Seljuk Turks as a formidable force in the Islamic world. Their triumph over the Byzantines at the Battle of Manzikert in 1071 was a turning point, leading to the gradual Seljuk Turkish occupation of Anatolia.

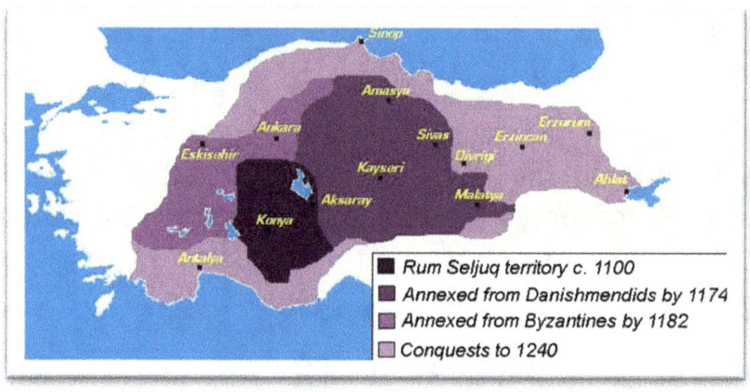

The Growth of the Anatolian Seljuk Sultanate

During the Seljuk era, Anatolia witnessed a fusion of cultures. The Seljuks brought their Turkic traditions, art, and architecture, influencing the Anatolian landscape. The renowned caravanserais along trade routes, such as the Sultan Han near Aksaray, reflected the Seljuk Turks' economic and cultural impact on the region.

The First Crusade, initiated by Pope Urban II in 1095, also impacted Anatolia, as Crusader armies traversed the region on their way to the Holy Land. This further complicated the political dynamics in Anatolia during this period.

The era marked by Arab invasions and conflicts with the Seljuk Turks played a vital role in shaping Anatolia's history. The Arab presence introduced new cultural and linguistic elements, while the Seljuk Turks left a lasting imprint on the region's political and architectural developments. These events set the stage for subsequent historical transformations in Anatolia, including the rise of the Seljuk Sultanate of Rum and interactions with the Crusader states.

Byzantine Empire's Governance in Turkey (Late Middle Emperor Heraclius (c. 575–641): Heraclius faced the challenge of the Arab invasions during his reign and played a significant role in the Byzantine response.

Battle of Yarmouk (636): A pivotal battle between the Byzantines and the Arab Caliphate, resulting in significant Arab victories and the capture of Jerusalem.

Arab Caliphates (7th century): The expansion of the Arab Caliphates, particularly the Umayyad and Abbasid Caliphates, had a profound impact on Anatolia.

Seljuk Turks (9th–11th centuries): The rise of the Seljuk Turks as a dominant force in the Islamic world, leading to conflicts with the Byzantines and the eventual victory at the Battle of Manzikert.

Battle of Manzikert (1071): A crucial battle where the Seljuk Turks, led by Alp Arslan, defeated the Byzantine Empire, marking a turning point in Anatolian history.

Sultanate of Rum (1077–1307): The establishment of the Sultanate of Rum after the Battle of Manzikert, shaping the political landscape of Anatolia.

Nicaea (İznik) and Antioch: Cities that fell to the Seljuks after the Battle of Manzikert, contributing to the reconfiguration of political boundaries in Anatolia.

First Crusade (1096–1099): Initiated by Pope Urban II, the First Crusade impacted Anatolia as Crusader armies traversed the region on their way to the Holy Land.

Caravanserais (e.g., Sultan Han near Aksaray): Reflecting the economic and cultural impact of the Seljuk Turks, caravanserais along trade routes played a crucial role in facilitating trade.

This period of Arab invasions and conflicts with the Seljuk Turks in Anatolia brought about significant political, cultural, and demographic changes, leaving a lasting imprint on the region's history. The interplay of these events shaped the dynamics of Anatolia and set the stage for subsequent historical developments.

The Mevlevi Order of dervishes, established in Konya during the 13th century by the Sufi poet Mevlânâ Rûmî, played a vital role in the Islamisation of Anatolia. The defeat of the Seljuks by the Mongols in 1243 led to the fragmentation of the Seljuk Sultanate of Rûm into smaller Turkish principalities.

The Mevlevi Order, also known as the Whirling Dervishes, holds a significant place in Anatolian history. Founded by Mevlânâ Rûmî, the order gained renown for its distinctive Sufi practices, including the iconic whirling dance symbolising spiritual ascent and union with the divine. Mevlânâ Rûmî's teachings, centred on love, tolerance, and spiritual enlightenment, contributed to the cultural and spiritual richness of Anatolia.

The Whirling Dervishes

The Seljuk defeat by the Mongols in 1243 had profound consequences for Anatolia, marking the end of centralised Seljuk rule and ushering in a period of political fragmentation. This era, often referred to as the Beylik period, witnessed the emergence of various Turkish beyliks, each vying for territorial control.

During this tumultuous period, the Mevlevi Order, with its emphasis on the spiritual and mystical aspects of Islam, played a role in shaping the religious and cultural landscape. Mevlânâ Rûmî's teachings resonated with many, providing solace and guidance amid political uncertainty.

The Battle of Manzikert in 1071 stands as a pivotal event that signalled Seljuk Turkish dominance in Anatolia and had far-reaching consequences for the Byzantine Empire.

This battle unfolded between the Byzantine Empire, led by Emperor Romanos IV Diogenes, and the Seljuk Turks, commanded by Alp Arslan. The Seljuks achieved a decisive victory, capturing Emperor Romanos IV and opening Anatolia to Seljuk expansion.

The aftermath of the Battle of Manzikert had profound implications for Anatolia. The defeat weakened the Byzantine hold on the region, enabling the Seljuk Turks to extend their influence and establish the Sultanate of Rum. Key cities like Nicaea (modern-day İznik) and Antioch fell to the Seljuks, reshaping the political landscape.

This marked a turning point in Byzantine history, leading to territorial losses and internal conflicts. The weakened central authority struggled to resist further Seljuk incursions.

Seljuk Turkish dominance introduced a new cultural and political era to Anatolia, bringing Turkic traditions, art, and architecture that influenced the region. The establishment of the Sultanate of Rum marked the beginning of a distinct political entity that endured for several centuries.

The Battle of Manzikert also had broader consequences, contributing to the dynamics of the Crusades as Western European powers sought to intervene. The weakened Byzantine Empire struggled to defend itself, ultimately leading to the Latin occupation of Constantinople during the Fourth Crusade in 1204.

The Battle of Manzikert was transformative, marking Seljuk Turkish dominance in Anatolia and shaping the course of Byzantine decline.

The period following the Battle of Manzikert, witnessing Seljuk Turkish dominance in Anatolia, was marked by notable cultural and architectural achievements. The arrival of the Seljuk Turks introduced Turkic cultural elements to Anatolia, blending with existing culture to create a unique synthesis.

The Seljuks fostered a rich intellectual environment, supporting Islamic scholarship. Anatolian cities became centres for learning, attracting scholars and theologians. The establishment of madrasahs contributed to knowledge dissemination. Turkish literature flourished, with notable poets and writers, including Sufi poet Yunus Emre, celebrated for spiritual depth.

Statue of the Poet Yunus Emre

In terms of architectural achievements, Seljuk architecture is renowned for mosques and religious buildings. The 13th-century Great Mosque of Konya exemplifies Seljuk style with intricate geometric patterns, calligraphy, and elegant domes.

The Seljuks contributed to educational institutions, combining educational and religious functions in medrese. The Gök Medrese in Sivas is an example. Seljuk architectural elements, reflecting Persian, Arab, and Central Asian influences, created a distinctive Anatolian style.

To address geopolitical challenges, the Seljuks constructed citadels and fortifications. Examples include Kayseri Castle and the Kayseri Grand Mosque Complex.

The Kayseri Grand Mosque Complex

The cultural and architectural achievements of the Seljuk period reflect a dynamic synthesis of various influences, laying the foundation for subsequent developments in Islamic art and architecture in Anatolia.

Alp Arslan (1029–1072): Alp Arslan was the Seljuk Sultan who led the Seljuks to victory in the Battle of Manzikert in 1071.

Romanos IV Diogenes (c. 1030–1072): Romanos IV Diogenes was the Byzantine Emperor defeated at the Battle of Manzikert.

Sultanate of Rum (1077–1307): Established after the Battle of Manzikert, the Sultanate of Rum was a Seljuk state in Anatolia.

Yunus Emre (c. 1238–1320): A renowned Sufi poet and mystic, Yunus Emre made significant contributions to Turkish literature during this period.

Mevlânâ Rûmî (1207–1273): The founder of the Mevlevi Order, Rûmî's teachings and poetry had a profound impact on Anatolian culture.

Great Mosque of Konya (13th century): An iconic mosque exemplifying Seljuk architecture with intricate geometric patterns and calligraphy.

Sultan Han (13th century): A caravanserai along trade routes, reflecting Seljuk architectural style and facilitating commerce.

Alay Han (13th century): Another significant caravanserai, contributing to trade and travel during the Seljuk era.

Gök Medrese in Sivas (13th century): An educational institution combining religious and educational functions, showcasing Seljuk architectural elements.

Kayseri Castle (13th century): A fortress constructed to address geopolitical challenges during the Seljuk period.

Kayseri Grand Mosque Complex (13th century): A religious and architectural complex in Kayseri, representing the Seljuk influence in the region.

Madrasahs (13th century): Educational institutions established during the Seljuk period, contributing to knowledge dissemination.

Latin Occupation of Constantinople (Fourth Crusade, 1204): The weakened Byzantine Empire fell to the Latin occupation during the Fourth Crusade, a consequence of the Battle of Manzikert.

These figures, places, and events provide a glimpse into the dynamic and transformative period of Seljuk Turkish dominance in Anatolia, marked by cultural, architectural, and geopolitical developments.

In 1299, the fledgling Ottoman Empire took its roots as Osman I established the Ottoman Beylik in the strategically positioned northwestern corner of Anatolia. Osman's astute leadership saw the principality expanding through strategic military campaigns and diplomatic alliances, capitalising on the weakened Seljuk Sultanate of Rum. Key battles, such as the Battle of Bapheus in 1302 and the momentous capture of Bursa in 1326, not only fortified Ottoman control but also marked the establishment of Bursa as the empire's inaugural capital.

Osman's rule laid the groundwork for the Ottoman Empire's administrative and military structures. The adoption of the title "Bey" by subsequent rulers underscored the autonomy of the Beylik. This title would later metamorphose into "Sultan" as the Ottoman state evolved in power. The introduction of the "millet" system allowed diverse communities within the empire, such as Greeks and Armenians, to maintain religious and cultural autonomy, contributing significantly to the empire's longevity.

Fast forward to 1453, Mehmed II, also known as Mehmed the Conqueror, ascended to the Ottoman throne in 1444 with a resolute goal — the conquest of Constantinople. Recognising the city's strategic importance as a bridge between Europe and Asia, as well as its rich cultural and historical significance, Mehmed II initiated the Ottoman siege of Constantinople in April 1453.

The protracted and intense campaign involved innovative military tactics, including the use of massive cannons like the famous "Basilica," ultimately breaching the formidable walls of Constantinople. The fall of the city on May 29, 1453, not only marked the end of the Byzantine Empire but also signified the rise of the Ottoman Empire as a major world power.

Mehmed II, (Mehmed the Conqueror)

Mehmed II's reign was characterised by a nuanced approach to cultural integration. The conversion of the iconic Hagia Sophia from a grand Byzantine cathedral to a mosque exemplified Mehmed II's desire to preserve the city's rich heritage while asserting Ottoman dominance. This cultural assimilation reflected the Ottomans' absorption of Byzantine traditions into their own, with the Hagia Sophia standing as a symbol of this synthesis.

Post-1453, the Ottoman Empire, under successive rulers, embarked on a vast and influential expansion across Europe, Asia, and Africa. In Europe, military campaigns and strategic alliances led to the Ottoman annexation of territories in southeastern Europe, including Greece, Bulgaria, and Serbia. The Battle of Mohács in 1526 further expanded Ottoman influence, resulting in the annexation of much of Hungary.

In Asia, Ottoman control extended into the Middle East, with Mesopotamia, the Levant, and parts of the Arabian Peninsula coming under Ottoman rule. Military campaigns against the Safavids in Persia and the Mamluks in Egypt expanded Ottoman influence in the region. The conquest of Egypt in 1517 solidified Ottoman control over crucial trade routes and facilitated naval access to the Red Sea.

The Ottoman Empire's incursions into North Africa saw the acquisition of Algiers and Tripoli, establishing a formidable presence along the Mediterranean coastline. This era of expansion brought about a cultural synthesis, evident in the diverse architectural styles of grand mosques, palaces, and public buildings constructed during this period, such as the iconic Topkapi Palace in Istanbul.

Topkapi Palace in Istanbul

While the Ottoman Empire reached its peak in the 16th and 17th centuries, internal strife, external pressures, and notable figures such as Suleiman the Magnificent contributed to its gradual decline. The empire persisted until the aftermath of World War I, when the Republic of Turkey emerged under Mustafa Kemal Atatürk.

The expansive legacy of the Ottoman Empire remains tangible today, evident in the diverse cultures, traditions, and architectural marvels that span three continents. The Ottomans left an indelible mark on the regions they governed, shaping the course of history and influencing the development of subsequent nations in Europe, Asia, and Africa.

Osman I (c. 1258–1326): Founder of the Ottoman Empire, Osman I established the Ottoman Beylik in 1299 in northwestern Anatolia. His military prowess and strategic alliances laid the foundation for Ottoman expansion.

Battle of Bapheus (1302): A significant early battle that fortified Ottoman control, allowing the principality to expand its influence in the wake of the weakened Seljuk Sultanate of Rum.

Capture of Bursa (1326): Marked the establishment of Bursa as the Ottoman Empire's first capital and solidified Ottoman dominance in the region.

Mehmed II (1432–1481): Known as Mehmed the Conqueror, he ascended to the throne in 1444 and achieved the historic conquest of Constantinople in 1453, marking the end of the Byzantine Empire.

Siege of Constantinople (1453): Mehmed II's strategic siege, including the use of massive cannons like the "Basilica," led to the fall of Constantinople, a pivotal moment in world history.

Cultural Integration: Mehmed II's nuanced approach to cultural assimilation, exemplified by the conversion of Hagia Sophia, showcased the Ottomans' absorption of Byzantine traditions into their own.

Ottoman Expansion in Europe (15th–16th centuries): Military campaigns and strategic alliances led to the annexation of territories in southeastern Europe, including Greece, Bulgaria, Serbia, and the Battle of Mohács in 1526 expanded Ottoman influence into much of Hungary.

Ottoman Control in the Middle East and North Africa: Ottoman expansion into the Middle East, with control over Mesopotamia, the Levant, and parts of the Arabian Peninsula, and conquests in North Africa, including Algiers and Tripoli.

Cultural Synthesis and Architecture: The Ottoman Empire's expansion brought about a cultural synthesis, reflected in diverse architectural styles seen in grand mosques, palaces, and public buildings, such as the iconic Topkapi Palace in Istanbul.

Suleiman the Magnificent (1494–1566): Notable Ottoman Sultan during the empire's golden age, known for military success, administrative reforms, and cultural patronage.

Ottoman Decline and World War I: Internal strife, external pressures, and challenges like those posed by Suleiman the Magnificent contributed to the gradual decline of the Ottoman Empire, which ultimately led to dissolution post World War I.

Legacy of the Ottoman Empire: The Ottoman legacy endures in diverse cultures, traditions, and architectural marvels across Europe, Asia, and Africa, influencing the development of subsequent nations and leaving an indelible mark on history.

The narrative progresses as we delve into the constitutional developments and administrative changes during the Tanzimat era in the Ottoman Empire.

The Tanzimat reforms, initiated in the mid-19th century, were a pivotal period marked by comprehensive changes aimed at modernising and restructuring various aspects of the Ottoman state. Constitutional and administrative reforms played a crucial role in reshaping the governance and legal frameworks of the empire.

A central focus of the Tanzimat era was the restructuring of the administrative system. The traditional feudal system gave way to a more centralised and meritocratic bureaucracy. Administrative divisions underwent rationalisation, and a streamlined hierarchy emerged to enhance the efficiency and responsiveness of the government.

Centralisation efforts were prominent during the Tanzimat reforms. Provincial governors were appointed centrally, and regulations were put in place to define their authority. This centralisation aimed to exert greater control over provincial administration, fostering uniformity in governance and facilitating more effective decision-making.

Legal reforms were integral to the Tanzimat era, with the introduction of the Mecelle, a civil code inspired by European legal principles. This reform sought to establish a standardised and impartial legal framework, ensuring equality before the law for all Ottoman subjects. It addressed issues ranging from property rights to family law, contributing to a more modern and equitable legal system.

Constitutional developments during the Tanzimat era laid the groundwork for future initiatives. The Hatt-i Sharif of Gülhane in 1839 and the Hatt-ı Hümayun of 1856 were early constitutional steps, emphasising principles of security, equality, and justice for Ottoman subjects. These laid the foundation for the more explicit constitutional attempts that followed.

In 1876, Sultan Abdulhamid II promulgated the Kanûn-ı Esâsî (Basic Law), marking the Ottoman Empire's first attempt at a written constitution. The constitution outlined principles of the separation of powers, fundamental rights, and the establishment of a consultative assembly, the Meclis-i Mebusan. However, its implementation was short-lived, facing suspension within two years.

Sultan Abdulhamid II

The Tanzimat reforms also showcased a nuanced approach to governance, balancing centralisation with attempts at decentralisation. The introduction of local councils, known as

Mecelle-i İdâre, aimed to involve local communities in decision-making processes. This reflected an effort to strike a balance between centralised control and local representation.

The constitutional and administrative changes implemented during the Tanzimat era laid the foundation for future constitutional developments in the Ottoman Empire. These reforms set the stage for more explicit constitutional initiatives in the late 19th and early 20th centuries, paving the way for subsequent transformative movements, such as those led by the Young Turks. The Ottoman Constitution of 1908, building upon the groundwork laid during the Tanzimat era, marked a significant milestone in the empire's journey towards modernisation and governance reform.

The Tanzimat era was a period of profound constitutional and administrative changes in the Ottoman Empire. These reforms aimed at modernising governance structures, ensuring legal equality, and adapting the administrative system to meet the challenges of the evolving global landscape. The legacy of the Tanzimat reforms resonated in subsequent constitutional developments that shaped the empire's trajectory in the late 19th and early 20th centuries.

Sultan Mahmud II (1785–1839): Initiated early reforms and laid the groundwork for Tanzimat.

Mustafa Reşit Pasha (1800–1858): A chief architect of the Tanzimat reforms, served as Grand Vizier.

Sultan Abdulmecid I (1823–1861): Implemented key reforms during his reign, including legal changes.

Sultan Abdulaziz (1830–1876): Continued Tanzimat reforms, faced challenges, and ultimately deposed.

Midhat Pasha (1822–1884): Played a crucial role in the formulation of the Kanûn-ı Esâsî (Basic Law).

Sultan Abdulhamid II (1842–1918): Promulgated the Kanûn-ı Esâsî, faced constitutional challenges.

Istanbul (Constantinople): The imperial capital, where many administrative and constitutional decisions were made.

Provincial Capitals: Various cities across the empire where administrative changes were implemented.

Local Councils (Mecelle-i İdâre): Local communities across the empire participated in decision-making.

Hatt-i Sharif of Gülhane (1839): Introduced principles of security, equality, and justice.

Hatt-ı Hümayun (1856): Further emphasised principles of equality and justice.

Promulgation of the Kanûn-ı Esâsî (1876): Ottoman Empire's first attempt at a written constitution.

Meclis-i Mebusan (1876): Establishment of a consultative assembly as part of the constitution.

The Tanzimat Legal Reforms: Introduction of the Mecelle, a civil code inspired by European legal principles.

The Ottoman Constitution of 1908: A significant milestone building upon Tanzimat era foundations.

These figures, places, and events played pivotal roles in shaping the course of the Tanzimat era, contributing to the constitutional and administrative transformations in the Ottoman Empire.

The establishment of a constitutional monarchy in 1876 represented a pivotal turning point in the political evolution of the Ottoman Empire. This era marked a departure from absolute monarchy, introducing principles of constitutional governance and representative government.

The Ottoman Constitution of 1876, encapsulated in the Kanûn-ı Esâsî or Basic Law, enshrined fundamental rights and liberties for Ottoman subjects. It addressed personal freedom, property rights, and equality before the law, providing a legal framework to safeguard individual rights. The constitution aimed to strike a balance by limiting the powers of the Sultan and subjecting the monarch's authority to the rule of law.

A crucial aspect of the constitutional framework was the separation of powers among the executive, legislative, and judicial branches. This system aimed to prevent the concentration of authority, fostering a system of checks and balances within the government.

While aspects of centralisation persisted, efforts were made to incorporate provincial representation. Local councils, known as Mecelle-i İdâre, were introduced to involve local communities in decision-making processes. This demonstrated a nuanced approach, attempting to balance centralised control with regional representation.

Despite the progressive ideals of the constitution, its implementation faced challenges. Sultan Abdulhamid II suspended the constitution in 1878, citing political instability and external threats. This suspension marked the beginning of a period of authoritarian rule, delaying the establishment of a sustained constitutional order.

The constitutional monarchy established in 1876 left a lasting legacy, symbolising the Ottoman Empire's attempts to modernise and adapt to evolving political ideologies. This period set the stage for subsequent constitutional initiatives, including the notable reestablishment of constitutional governance with the Young Turk Revolution in 1908.

Fast forward to the Young Turk Revolution of 1908, an event that brought about further transformative reforms in the Ottoman Empire. The restoration of constitutional governance following the revolution aimed to address demands for political liberalisation and representation.

The Committee of Union and Progress (CUP), popularly known as the Young Turks, played a central role in this revolution. Their agenda included modernising the empire, fostering national unity, and responding to internal and external challenges. The reinstatement of the Ottoman Constitution in 1908 marked the commencement of the Second Constitutional Era, emphasising principles of representative government and individual rights.

The Young Turks implemented a series of reforms to centralise and modernise the political structure. The legal system underwent significant changes with the introduction of the Ottoman Civil Code of 1917, aligning it with modern principles and aiming to enhance legal equality.

The Young Turk Revolution of 1908

Educational reforms were prioritised, with an emphasis on establishing secular schools, promoting scientific education, and improving overall educational standards. Language reforms also took place, simplifying and modernising the Ottoman Turkish script, culminating in the adoption of a modified version of the Latin alphabet in 1928.

The Young Turks advocated for Ottoman nationalism, seeking to unite the diverse ethnic and religious groups within the empire. However, challenges emerged, and ethno-nationalist movements gained prominence in later years. The geopolitical complexities of World War I strained the empire's resources, contributing to its eventual dissolution.

The Young Turk Revolution of 1908 caused a period of comprehensive reforms in the Ottoman Empire, covering political, legal, educational, and linguistic genres. The Young Turks' vision of modernisation and national unity left an impact on the empire's trajectory, shaping later years and influencing the formation of successor states after World War I.

Sultan Abdulhamid II (1842–1918): Suspended the Ottoman Constitution of 1876, leading to a period of authoritarian rule.

Committee of Union and Progress (CUP): Popularly known as the Young Turks, played a central role in the Young Turk Revolution of 1908.

Leaders of the Young Turk Revolution: Talat Pasha, Enver Pasha, and Ahmed Djemal Pasha were key figures in the revolutionary movement.

Architects of Ottoman Legal Reforms: Those involved in drafting and implementing the Ottoman Civil Code of 1917.

Istanbul (Constantinople): The political and cultural heart of the Ottoman Empire, where constitutional decisions were made.

Representation Halls: Venues for political discussions and decisions during the constitutional monarchy and the Young Turk period.

Educational Institutions: Focus of reforms, including the establishment of secular schools.

Establishment of Constitutional Monarchy (1876): Adoption of the Ottoman Constitution (Kanûn-ı Esâsî) represented a shift towards constitutional governance.

Suspension of the Constitution (1878): Sultan Abdulhamid II suspended the constitution, leading to a period of authoritarian rule.

Young Turk Revolution (1908): Marked the restoration of constitutional governance, initiating the Second Constitutional Era.

Introduction of the Ottoman Civil Code (1917): Significant legal reform aligning the legal system with modern principles.

Adoption of the Latin Alphabet (1928): Culmination of language reforms, replacing the Ottoman Turkish script with a modified Latin alphabet.

Secular School Reforms: Emphasis on establishing secular schools and improving overall educational standards.

Language Reforms: Simplification and modernisation of the Ottoman Turkish script, leading to the adoption of the Latin alphabet in 1928.

Authoritarian Rule (1878–1908): The suspension of the constitution by Sultan Abdulhamid II led to a period of centralised authority.

Geopolitical Complexities of World War I: Strained resources and contributed to the dissolution of the Ottoman Empire.

The figures, places, and events during the establishment of the constitutional monarchy in 1876 and the Young Turk Revolution of 1908 played crucial roles in shaping the political evolution of the Ottoman Empire during these transformative periods.

From the latter half of the 18th century onwards, the Ottoman Empire experienced a decline that prompted Mahmud II to initiate the Tanzimat reforms in 1839. These reforms aimed to modernise the Ottoman state in alignment with Western European progress. Although Midhat Pasha's efforts during the late Tanzimat era led to the constitutional movement of 1876 and the introduction of the First Constitutional Era, the decline persisted, ultimately resulting in the dissolution of the empire.

As the empire contracted in size, military power waned, and wealth dwindled, events such as the Ottoman economic crisis and default in 1875 triggered uprisings in the Balkan provinces, leading to the Russo-Turkish War (1877–1878). Many Balkan Muslims migrated to Anatolia, accompanied by Circassians fleeing the Russian conquest of the Caucasus. The decline also fuelled nationalist sentiments among various subject peoples, contributing to ethnic tensions and instances of violence, such as the Hamidian massacres of Armenians.

The loss of Rumelia (Ottoman territories in Europe) during the First Balkan War (1912–1913) prompted the arrival of millions of Muslim refugees to Istanbul and Anatolia. The subsequent Ottoman coup d'état in 1913 marked a significant shift in the empire's governance, placing the country under the control of the Three Pashas, rendering sultans Mehmed V and Mehmed VI as symbolic figureheads with minimal political power.

The Hamidian Massacres of Armenians

World War I saw the Ottoman Empire aligning with the Central Powers, defending the Dardanelles strait successfully during the Gallipoli campaign but facing defeats in the Mesopotamian and Caucasus campaigns. The Armenian genocide occurred during the war, resulting in the deportation and death of a significant number of Armenians, along with genocidal campaigns against other minority groups like the Assyrians and Greeks.

Following the Armistice of Mudros in 1918, the victorious Allied Powers sought to partition the Ottoman Empire through the 1920 Treaty of Sèvres.

The aftermath of World War I saw the occupation of Istanbul (1918) and İzmir (1919) by the Allies, sparking the Turkish National Movement led by Mustafa Kemal Pasha. The Turkish War of Independence (1919–1923) aimed to annul the Treaty of Sèvres (1920). The Turkish Provisional Government in Ankara, established on 23 April 1920, formalised the transition from the Ottoman to the new Republican political system. The military and diplomatic efforts of the Ankara Government resulted in the expulsion of Armenian, Greek, French, and British forces by 1923. The Armistice of Mudanya (1922) and the handling of the Chanak Crisis led to the signing of the Treaty of Lausanne (1923), ending the Ottoman Sultanate on 1 November 1922 and recognising the sovereignty of the new Turkish state.

The Signing of the Treaty of Lausanne (1923)

The height and subsequent decline of the Ottoman Empire were marked by territorial losses, internal reforms, and geopolitical shifts. The Ottoman Empire's cultural and demographic landscape was shaped by events such as the influx of refugees, the Tanzimat reforms, and the ethnic tensions that contributed to the empire's eventual dissolution.

The Ottoman Empire's participation in World War I, spanning from 1914 to 1918, marked a significant and transformative period with far-reaching consequences for the empire's destiny.

Facing internal challenges and seeking international strength, the Ottoman Empire, under the rule of the Committee of Union and Progress (CUP), aligned itself with the Central Powers— Germany and Austria-Hungary. Ottoman forces engaged in various theatres of war, including the Caucasus Campaign against Russia, the successful defence of the Dardanelles in the Gallipoli Campaign, and campaigns in Mesopotamia against the British.

One tragic aspect of this period was the Armenian Genocide, a systematic campaign resulting in the mass deportation and killing of Armenians. The Ottoman Empire's involvement in World War I strained its resources, exacerbated economic challenges, and contributed to internal unrest, leading to discontent among its diverse ethnic and religious groups.

As the war turned against the Central Powers, the Ottoman Empire signed the Armistice of Mudros on October 30, 1918, marking the end of its involvement in World War I. The subsequent Treaty of Sèvres in 1920 imposed significant territorial losses on the Ottoman Empire, further sealing its fate and setting the stage for the emergence of the Republic of Turkey under Mustafa Kemal Atatürk.

Mustafa Kemal Atatürk's leadership during the War of Independence, following World War I, was a pivotal moment in Turkish history. Faced with Allied occupation and the partitioning of Turkish territories as per the Treaty of Sèvres, Atatürk emerged as a leader rallying against foreign intervention.

In response, Mustafa Kemal convened the Grand National Assembly in Ankara in 1920, symbolising a nationalist movement committed to resisting foreign occupation. The War of Independence officially began, marked by crucial battles such as the Battle of Sakarya and the Great Offensive.

Mustafa Kemal's strategic brilliance and leadership culminated in decisive victories, notably the Battle of Dumlupınar in August 1922, leading to the retreat and defeat of Greek forces. The success of the War of Independence laid the groundwork for the Treaty of Lausanne in 1923, replacing the Treaty of Sèvres and establishing the Republic of Turkey as a sovereign state with defined borders.

On October 29, 1923, Mustafa Kemal Atatürk officially declared the establishment of the Republic of Turkey and became its first President. His leadership during the War of Independence and subsequent reforms, known as the Kemalist reforms, transformed Turkey into a modern, secular nation-state.

The Ottoman Empire's involvement in World War I and Mustafa Kemal Atatürk's leadership during the War of Independence represent two pivotal chapters that shaped the trajectory of Turkey's history. These events, marked by war, resistance, and visionary leadership, laid the foundation for the emergence of the modern Republic of Turkey.

Mustafa Kemal Atatürk

Mahmud II (1785–1839): Initiated the Tanzimat reforms in 1839 in response to the Ottoman Empire's decline.

Midhat Pasha (1822–1884): Played a key role in the late Tanzimat era, contributing to the constitutional movement of 1876.

Mustafa Kemal Atatürk (1881–1938): Led the Turkish National Movement during the War of Independence and founded the Republic of Turkey.

Istanbul: Capital of the Ottoman Empire, witnessed significant events during the decline, constitutional movements, and occupation.

Ankara: Became the centre of resistance during the War of Independence and the capital of the new Republic of Turkey.

Gallipoli: Site of the successful Ottoman defence during the Gallipoli Campaign in World War I.

Tanzimat Reforms (1839): Initiated by Mahmud II to modernise the Ottoman state in response to its decline.

Constitutional Movement of 1876: Midhat Pasha's efforts led to the First Constitutional Era, aiming to address governance issues.

Russo-Turkish War (1877–1878): Triggered by uprisings in the Balkans, resulting in territorial losses.

First Balkan War (1912–1913): Further territorial losses in Rumelia, leading to the arrival of Muslim refugees.

Ottoman Coup d'État (1913): Shifted governance, placing the Three Pashas in control and diminishing the sultans' power.

World War I (1914–1918): Ottoman Empire aligned with the Central Powers, facing defeat, economic crisis, and the Armenian Genocide.

Armistice of Mudros (1918): Ended Ottoman involvement in World War I.

Turkish War of Independence (1919–1923): Led by Mustafa Kemal Atatürk, resulting in the establishment of the Republic of Turkey.

Treaty of Sèvres (1920): Imposed significant territorial losses on the Ottoman Empire.

Treaty of Lausanne (1923): Recognised the sovereignty of the new Republic of Turkey and ended the Ottoman Sultanate.

Influx of Refugees: Migration of Balkan Muslims and Circassians to Anatolia during territorial losses.

Ethnic Tensions: Nationalist sentiments and tensions among diverse subject peoples, contributing to violence and massacres.

Gallipoli Campaign (1915–1916): Successful Ottoman defence against Allied forces.

Caucasus Campaign: Ottoman engagement against Russia during World War I.

Mesopotamian Campaign: Ottoman campaigns against the British during World War I.

Mustafa Kemal Atatürk's Leadership: Led the War of Independence, founded the Republic of Turkey, and implemented Kemalist reforms.

These figures, places, and events shaped the Ottoman Empire's decline, its participation in World War I, and the subsequent

The official proclamation of the Turkish Republic on 29 October 1923 in Ankara marked a pivotal moment in Turkish history. Mustafa Kemal Atatürk, the leader of the successful War of Independence, assumed the presidency, and Ankara replaced Istanbul as the capital. The construction of Anıtkabir as Atatürk's mausoleum underscored the significance of this historical transition. Atatürk's subsequent reforms aimed to establish a secular parliamentary republic, leading to discontent and rebellions in Kurdish and Zaza tribes. İsmet İnönü succeeded Atatürk in 1938 and oversaw the integration of the Republic of Hatay in 1939.

Turkey entered World War II on the side of the Allies in 1945, joined the United Nations, and became a Council of Europe member in 1950. After participating in the Korean War, Turkey joined NATO in 1952.

The transition to multi-party democracy in 1950 was a landmark development in Turkey's political landscape. After years of single-party rule under the Republican People's Party (CHP), led by Mustafa Kemal Atatürk and İsmet İnönü, the country embraced a multi-party system. The Democratic Party (DP), led by Adnan Menderes, emerged victorious in the 1950 elections, leading to a peaceful transfer of power. Adnan Menderes became the Prime Minister, and Celal Bayar assumed the presidency. This transition allowed for greater political representation, diversity of voices, and competitive elections.

Under Mustafa Kemal Atatürk's leadership, a series of comprehensive reforms were initiated to modernise and secularise Turkey, transforming it into a modern nation-state. These reforms included the abolition of the Ottoman Sultanate, the introduction of a multiparty system, the adoption of a new constitution, the replacement of Islamic law, the introduction of a civil code, the introduction of a new alphabet, and the secularisation of education. Atatürk's vision also encompassed language reforms, the promotion of Turkish identity, industrialisation initiatives, land reforms, Westernisation, and the promotion of secularism.

In the latter half of the 20th century, Turkey experienced political interruptions with military coups in 1960 and 1980, as well as memorandums in 1971 and 1997. Key political figures during this period included Süleyman Demirel, Bülent Ecevit, Turgut Özal, and Tansu Çiller, who became Turkey's first female prime minister in 1993. Turkey sought European Economic Community (EEC) membership in 1987, joined the European Union Customs Union in 1995, and began EU accession negotiations in 2005. The European Parliament called for a suspension of accession talks in 2019, but negotiations remain active.

Recep Tayyip Erdoğan won Turkey's first direct presidential election in 2014. The unsuccessful coup attempt in 2016 was followed by a 2017 referendum that replaced the parliamentary republic with an executive presidential system, abolishing the office of the prime minister and transferring its powers to the president. The opposition raised concerns about ballot validity during the referendum.

Tansu Çiller, Turkey's First Female Prime Minister in 1993

Turkey's journey from the proclamation of the Turkish Republic in 1923, through the transition to multi-party democracy in 1950, the comprehensive reforms under Mustafa Kemal Atatürk, and the political developments in the latter half of the 20th century, reflects a dynamic and transformative history that has shaped the country's political, social, and cultural identity.

Mustafa Kemal Atatürk (1881–1938): Leader of the War of Independence, founder of the Turkish Republic, and its first President.

İsmet İnönü (1884–1973): Succeeded Atatürk as President in 1938, oversaw the integration of the Republic of Hatay, and led during World War II.

Adnan Menderes (1899–1961): Leader of the Democratic Party, became Prime Minister after the transition to multi-party democracy in 1950.

Ankara: Replaced Istanbul as the capital after the proclamation of the Turkish Republic in 1923.

Anıtkabir: Mausoleum built in Ankara as the final resting place of Mustafa Kemal Atatürk, symbolising the historical transition.

Proclamation of the Turkish Republic (1923): Mustafa Kemal Atatürk assumes the presidency, Ankara becomes the capital, and comprehensive reforms are initiated.

Transition to Multi-Party Democracy (1950): Democratic Party led by Adnan Menderes wins elections, marking a shift from single-party rule.

Integration of the Republic of Hatay (1939): İsmet İnönü oversees the incorporation of Hatay into the Turkish Republic.

Turkey Joins World War II (1945): Becomes an Allied Power, joins the United Nations, and later becomes a member of the Council of Europe in 1950.

Korean War (1950–1953): Turkey participates and joins NATO in 1952.

Military Coups and Memorandums (1960, 1971, 1980, 1997): Periods of political interruptions and interventions.

European Union Relations (1987–Present): Seeks EEC membership, joins the EU Customs Union in 1995, and starts accession negotiations in 2005.

Recep Tayyip Erdoğan's Presidency (2014–Present): Wins Turkey's first direct presidential election in 2014, followed by constitutional changes in 2017.

Süleyman Demirel: A prominent political figure involved in various governments and multiple presidencies.

Bülent Ecevit: Prime Minister and political figure, known for his contributions during various periods.

Turgut Özal: Key figure in the 1980s, serving as Prime Minister and later as President.

Tansu Çiller: Turkey's first female Prime Minister in 1993.

Recep Tayyip Erdoğan's Leadership: Wins the first direct presidential election in 2014, introduces constitutional changes in 2017.

2016 Coup Attempt: Unsuccessful military intervention followed by political purges.

2017 Referendum: Shifts from a parliamentary republic to an executive presidential system.

This dynamic and transformative history reflects Turkey's journey from its founding in 1923 through political shifts, reforms, and challenges that have shaped its modern identity.

The period from 2017 to the present has been marked by significant events that have shaped Turkey's trajectory on the global stage. Under the leadership of President Recep Tayyip Erdoğan, the country has faced numerous challenges and witnessed both domestic and international developments that have influenced its political, social, and economic landscape.

President Recep Tayyip Erdoğan

In 2017, Turkey underwent a constitutional referendum that fundamentally altered its political structure. The proposed changes sought to replace the parliamentary system with a presidential one, concentrating executive powers in the hands of the president. Despite concerns raised by opposition groups about the implications for democracy, the referendum passed, leading to the adoption of the executive presidential system.

This constitutional shift abolished the office of the prime minister and granted the president enhanced executive authority, including the ability to issue decrees with the force of law, appoint ministers, and dissolve the parliament. The changes aimed to streamline decision-making processes but also raised questions about the checks and balances within the government.

The implementation of the executive presidential system brought about notable changes in Turkey's political landscape. President Erdoğan, having won the first direct presidential election in 2014, continued to play a central role in shaping the country's policies and direction. The transition sparked debates about the balance of power and the state of democracy in Turkey, with critics expressing concerns about the concentration of authority.

One of the defining moments during this period was the attempted coup on July 15, 2016. Elements within the military sought to overthrow the government, leading to a night of unrest and clashes across the country. President Erdoğan's prompt response, rallying public support, and a decisive crackdown against coup plotters marked a turning point. The aftermath saw a series of purges, arrests, and legal proceedings, raising international concerns about human rights.

The Attempted Coup in 2016

In the wake of the coup attempt, a state of emergency was declared, granting the government extraordinary powers. The state of emergency continued until 2018 and had a profound impact on the country's institutions and civil society. Mass dismissals, arrests, and changes in legislation heightened tensions and led to debates about the balance between security concerns and individual freedoms.

Turkey's foreign policy has been dynamic, with active involvement in regional conflicts and evolving diplomatic relations. The conflict in Syria, particularly the Syrian Civil War, has been a focal point. Turkey's military interventions, including

Operation Olive Branch in Afrin and Operation Peace Spring in northeastern Syria, aimed at addressing security concerns and influencing the political landscape in the region.

Diplomatically, Turkey has navigated a complex relationship with the European Union (EU) and faced challenges such as disagreements over migration, human rights, and the accession process. Tensions with some NATO allies, particularly the United States, have also shaped Turkey's foreign relations.

The economic landscape of Turkey has witnessed both successes and challenges during this period. Positive economic growth, infrastructure projects, and efforts to attract foreign investment have been notable achievements. However, economic downturns, currency fluctuations, and inflation have posed challenges impacting the lives of ordinary citizens and contributing to debates about economic policies.

Social and cultural dynamics in Turkey have evolved, reflecting changing attitudes, generational shifts, and global influences. Debates about identity, secularism, and religious expression continue to shape societal discussions. Women's rights, LGBTQ+ rights, and freedom of expression have been subjects of ongoing discourse, highlighting the diversity of perspectives within Turkish society.

Reforms in the education sector have aimed at aligning the curriculum with national values and global standards. Technological advances and digital transformation have played a significant role in shaping communication, media, and access to information.

The period from 2017 to the present represents a chapter in Turkey's history marked by a complex interplay of political, economic, social, and cultural dynamics. As the country navigates challenges and opportunities, the ongoing discourse about the balance between security and individual rights, the role of democracy, and Turkey's place in the global community continues to shape its identity in the 21st century.

Recep Tayyip Erdoğan: President of Turkey since 2014, central in shaping political, economic, and foreign policy decisions.

Key Opposition Figures: Leaders of opposition parties and civil society figures contributing to political debates and movements.

Military Leaders: Figures involved in the response to the 2016 attempted coup, shaping military policies and actions.

Constitutional Referendum (2017): Transitioned to an executive presidential system, concentrating power in the hands of the president.

July 15, 2016, Coup Attempt: Attempted military overthrow, leading to a state of emergency and significant political repercussions.

State of Emergency (2016–2018): Implemented in the aftermath of the coup attempt, impacting institutions and civil society.

Military Interventions in Syria: Operations such as Operation Olive Branch and Operation Peace Spring aimed at addressing security concerns.

Foreign Relations Challenges: Complex relations with the European Union and tensions with NATO allies, particularly the United States.

Economic Dynamics: Positive growth, infrastructure projects, but also challenges such as economic downturns, currency fluctuations, and inflation.

Social and Cultural Changes: Evolving attitudes, debates about identity, secularism, and human rights issues, including women's and LGBTQ+ rights.

Education Reforms: Changes in the education sector to align curriculum with national values and global standards.

Technological Advances: Impact of digital transformation on communication, media, and access to information.

Balance of Power: Debates about the concentration of authority in the executive presidential system.

Human Rights Concerns: International scrutiny over purges, arrests, and changes in legislation after the coup attempt.

Foreign Policy Complexities: Managing relationships with the EU, NATO allies, and involvement in regional conflicts.

Economic Issues: Balancing economic growth with challenges like currency fluctuations and inflation.

Social and Cultural Discourse: Ongoing discussions about identity, secularism, and rights issues within Turkish society.

Education and Technology: Reforms in education and the impact of technological advances on societal dynamics.

The period from 2017 to the present has been characterised by a dynamic interplay of political, economic, social, and cultural factors that continue to shape Turkey's trajectory on the global stage. As the country faces challenges and embraces opportunities, the ongoing discourse reflects the complexity of issues such as democracy, human rights, and Turkey's role in the international community.

.

A TIMELINE OF TURKEY'S HISTORY

PREHISTORIC ANATOLIA

(BEFORE 2000 B.C.)

Settlements dating back to the Paleolithic era, with evidence of human habitation in areas like Çatalhöyük.

Hittite Empire emerges around 1600 B.C., establishing a powerful Anatolian state with a notable capital, Hattusa.

ANCIENT ANATOLIA

(1000 B.C. - 330 A.D.)

Rise of the Phrygians, known for their distinctive architecture, and the wealthy Lydians, famous for their use of coinage.

Alexander the Great conquers Anatolia in 334 B.C., bringing Greek influence to the region.

Roman Empire absorbs Anatolia in 133 B.C., incorporating it into the province of Asia.

BYZANTINE ERA

(330 - 1453)

Constantinople becomes the capital in 330 CE, serving as a centre for trade, culture, and Christianity.

The region plays a key role in the early Christian Church, with significant theological developments and the construction of iconic churches like Hagia Sophia.

Arab and Seljuk invasions impact the Byzantine Empire, leading to territorial losses and political challenges.

SELJUK AND OTTOMAN PERIOD

(1071 - 1922)

Battle of Manzikert in 1071 sees the Seljuks defeating the Byzantines, opening Anatolia to Turkish migration.

Osman I founds the Ottoman Empire in the early 14th century, with the capital initially at Bursa.

Conquest of Constantinople in 1453 by Mehmed II marks the end of the Byzantine Empire.

Ottoman Empire reaches its height under Suleiman the Magnificent, expanding into Europe, Asia, and Africa.

Decline and reform efforts in the 17th and 18th centuries, including the Tulip Period and efforts to modernize the military and administration.

MODERNISATION AND DECLINE

(19TH CENTURY)

Tanzimat reforms in the mid-19th century aim to modernize the Ottoman state, introducing legal and administrative changes.

Ottoman Empire faces challenges, including nationalist movements among various ethnic and religious groups.

WORLD WAR I AND THE TURKISH WAR OF INDEPENDENCE

(1914 - 1923)

Ottoman Empire sides with the Central Powers in World War I, leading to its partition and occupation by Allied forces.

Mustafa Kemal Atatürk leads the Turkish War of Independence (1919-1922), resisting foreign occupation and establishing a nationalist movement.

Republic of Turkey is declared in 1923, with Ankara as the new capital, and Atatürk becomes the first president.

ATATÜRK'S REFORMS AND MODERN TURKEY

(1923 - 1938)

Atatürk introduces significant political, social, and cultural reforms, including the adoption of a new legal code and the introduction of the Latin alphabet.

Turkey becomes a secular republic, separating religion from the state and encouraging a modern, Western-oriented outlook.

POST-ATATÜRK ERA

(1938 - PRESENT)

Multi-party democracy is established in 1950, marking a shift from the early single-party system.

Turkey joins NATO in 1952, aligning itself with Western security interests during the Cold War.

Economic and political challenges in the latter half of the 20th century, including periods of military intervention.

Relations with the European Union, economic growth, and political changes in the 21st century, with ongoing discussions about Turkey's role in the international community.

Mustafa Kemal Atatürk (1881–1938):

Role: Founder and first President of the Republic of Turkey.

Notes: Led the War of Independence, initiated the Kemalist reforms, established the Republic in 1923, and implemented secular and modernizing policies.

İsmet İnönü (1884–1973):

Role: Second President of Turkey.

Notes: Succeeded Atatürk, led during the single-party period, and transitioned Turkey to a multi-party system after World War II.

Celal Bayar (1883–1986):

Role: Third President of Turkey.

Notes: Served as the first democratically elected president, contributing to the country's economic development.

Cemal Gürsel (1895–1966):

Role: Fourth President of Turkey.

Notes: Oversaw the transition to a multi-party system, faced political unrest, and briefly served as the Prime Minister.

Cevdet Sunay (1899–1982):

Role: Fifth President of Turkey.

Notes: Addressed political challenges during his presidency and promoted economic stability.

Süleyman Demirel (1924–2015):

Role: Prime Minister multiple times, Ninth President of Turkey.

Notes: Known for his contributions to infrastructure projects, economic reforms, and political leadership during various periods.

Bülent Ecevit (1925–2006):

Role: Multiple terms as Prime Minister.

Notes: Led during critical periods, including the 1974 Cyprus intervention, and implemented social and economic reforms.

Kenan Evren (1917–2015):

Role: Seventh President of Turkey.

Notes: Led the 1980 military coup, served as president during the transition to civilian rule, and played a role in constitutional changes.

Turgut Özal (1927–1993):

Role: Eighth President of Turkey.

Notes: Implemented economic liberalisation policies, initiated infrastructure projects, and contributed to Turkey's regional influence.

Süleyman Demirel (1924–2015) - Second Term:

Role: Eighth President of Turkey (second term).

Notes: Returned to the presidency for a second term after serving as Prime Minister multiple times.

Ahmet Necdet Sezer (1941–):

Role: Tenth President of Turkey.

Notes: Known for his emphasis on the rule of law, judiciary independence, and served during a period of political and economic challenges.

Abdullah Gül (1950–):

Role: Eleventh President of Turkey.

Notes: First president with an Islamist background, contributed to Turkey's diplomatic efforts, and supported EU accession.

Recep Tayyip Erdoğan (1954–):

Role: Current President of Turkey.

Notes: Former Prime Minister, leading figure in the AKP, implemented constitutional changes, and faced both domestic and international challenges.

This list covers key leaders and rulers of Turkey from its founding to the present, highlighting their roles and contributions to the country's political, economic, and social development.

INFLUENTIAL PEOPLE IN TURKEY'S HISTORY ACROSS GENRES

1. Mustafa Kemal Atatürk (1881–1938):

Genre: Politics, Military, Statecraft.

Founder of the Republic of Turkey, led the War of Independence, initiated Kemalist reforms, established a secular state, and modernised Turkey.

2. Rumi (Jalāl al-Dīn Muḥammad Rūmī) (1207–1273):

Genre: Poetry, Mysticism, Philosophy.

Influential Sufi mystic and poet, founder of the Mevlevi Order (Whirling Dervishes), his works transcend cultures and continue to inspire.

3. Hacı Bektaş Veli (1209–1271):

Genre: Philosophy, Sufism.

Philosopher and Sufi saint, founder of the Bektaşi order, known for promoting tolerance, equality, and humanism.

4. Sabiha Gökçen (1913–2001):

Genre: Aviation.

World's first female combat pilot, adopted daughter of Atatürk, and a symbol of women's empowerment in Turkey.

5. Orhan Pamuk (1952–):

Genre: Literature, Nobel Prize Winner.

Renowned novelist, recipient of the Nobel Prize in Literature, known for works exploring Turkey's history, culture, and identity.

6. Mimar Sinan (1489–1588):

Genre: Architecture.

Ottoman chief architect, designed iconic structures like the Süleymaniye Mosque, contributed significantly to Ottoman architecture.

7. Fatih Sultan Mehmet (Mehmed the Conqueror) (1432–1481):

Genre: Military, Politics.

Conqueror of Constantinople in 1453, expanded the Ottoman Empire, and played a crucial role in shaping its destiny.

8. Yunus Emre (1238–1320):

Genre: Poetry, Mysticism.

Influential Turkish poet and Sufi mystic, his poetry focused on love, tolerance, and spiritual enlightenment.

9. Fazıl Say (1970–):

Genre: Music, Classical Pianist, Composer.

Internationally acclaimed pianist and composer, known for blending Western classical music with Turkish influences.

10. Atıf Yılmaz (1925–2006):

Genre: Cinema, Film Directing. - Pioneering Turkish film director, contributed to Turkish cinema with a vast array of films, shaping the industry.

11. Türkan Saylan (1935–2009):

Genre: Medicine, Activism. - Renowned dermatologist and women's rights activist, founded the Turkish Association for the Fight Against Leprosy, known for her philanthropy.

12. Necmettin Erbakan (1926–2011):

Genre: Politics, Islamic Thought. - First Islamist Prime Minister of Turkey, founder of the Welfare Party, played a significant role in shaping political discourse.

This list encompasses influential figures from various domains, including politics, literature, arts, philosophy, and activism, who have left a lasting impact on Turkey's history and cultural landscape.

Index

IMAGE CREDITS

Picture Title	Credit Attributions
The Emblem of Turkey	Deviantart.com
The Flag of Turkey	CIA World Factbook, Public domain, via Wikimedia Commons
Map of Turkey in Europe	www.maps-of-the-world.net
The Göbekli Tepe Stone Pillars	Teomancimit, via Wikimedia Commons
Alexander the Great Cutting the Gordian Knot	Martino Altomonte, Public domain, via Wikimedia Commons
Altar of Zeus in Pergamon	Mark Landon (photographed in 1991; digitised in 2021) via Wikimedia Commons
Mithridates VI	Sting, via Wikimedia Commons
Burial Site of Apostle John in Ephesus	Levork (Julian Fong), via Wikimedia Commons
Medallion of Constantine the Great	NAC, via Wikimedia Commons
Roman General Lucius Cornelius Sulla	Rijksmuseum, CC0, via Wikimedia Commons
Hagia Sophia in Constantinople	Torcy, France, via Wikimedia Commons
Map of Constantinople in 1572	Georg Braun & Frans Hogenberg, Public domain, via Wikimedia Commons
The Growth of the Anatolian Seljuk Sultanate	Tiger23, Public domain, via Wikimedia Commons
The Whirling Dervishes	Britten, via Wikimedia Commons
Statue of the Poet Yunus Emre	Dosseman, via Wikimedia Commons
The Kayseri Grand Mosque Complex	Abdurrahman Çam, via Wikimedia Commons
Mehmed II, (Mehmed the Conqueror)	Konstantin Kapıdağlı, Public domain, via Wikimedia Commons
Topkapi Palace in Istanbul	Public domain, via Wikimedia Commons
Sultan Abdulhamid II	George Grantham Bain Collection, Public domain, via Wikimedia Commons
The Young Turk Revolution of 1908	Илюстрация Илинден, 1930, бр. 28, стр.13, Public domain, via Wikimedia Commons
The Hamidian Massacres of Armenians	"Turkey and the Armenian Atrocities" by Rev. Edwin M. BlissEdgewood Publishing Company, 1896, p. 306, Public domain, via Wikimedia Commons
The Signing of the Treaty of Lausanne (1923)	Hub Pages, Public domain, via Wikimedia Commons
Mustafa Kemal Atatürk	Public domain, via Wikimedia Commons
Tansu Çiller, Turkey's First Female Prime Minister in 1993	Thierry Dauwe, European Communities, Attribution, via Wikimedia Commons
President Recep Tayyip Erdoğan	President.az, via Wikimedia Commons
The Attempted Coup in 2016	Gleseek, via Wikimedia Commons

Martin Miller-Yianni, a London native born in 1958, emerged from a humble working-class background. Despite starting his career as a primary school teacher, an unexpected turn of events led him to venture into Southeastern Europe in 2005. Since then, Martin has fully embraced the unique way of life and culture of the region, igniting a passion for writing within him.

Having served as a journalist and researcher for a leading information website about this area, he has developed a profound knowledge, understanding, and first-hand experience of this part of the world.

Martin's intimate connection with Southeastern Europe, rooted in both personal and professional experiences, continues to inspire and influence his literary pursuits.

His latest literary work on Turkey is a testament to his deep appreciation and admiration for the region's rich and captivating heritage.